A CHILD'S DAY
IN A PERUVIAN CITY

Para los niños huamanguinos que fueron mi padre y mi tío Renan,
también para Jesús y Ximena, y los demas niños de Huamanga

Copyright © Frances Lincoln Limited 2002
Text and photographs copyright © Sara Andrea Fajardo 2002
First published in Great Britain in 2002 by Frances Lincoln Limited
First American Edition, 2003

Benchmark Books
Marshall Cavendish
99 White Plains Road
Tarrytown, New York 10591
www.marshallcavendish.com

Library of Congress Cataloging-in-Publication Data

Fajardo, Sara Andrea.
In a Peruvian city / by Sara Andrea Fajardo.— 1st American ed.
p. cm. — (A child's day)
Includes index.
Summary: Presents a day in the life of a child living in Ayacucho, discussing the
social life, customs, religion, history, and language of Peru.
ISBN 0-7614-1408-8
1. Ayacucho (Peru)—Social life and customs—Juvenile literature.
2. Children—Peru—Ayacucho—Juvenile literature. 3. City and town
life—Peru—Ayacucho—Juvenile literature. [1. Peru—Social life and
customs.] I. Title. II. Series.
F3611.A9 F34 2002   985'.2925—dc21   2001052442

Designed by Sophie Pelham

Printed in Singapore

3 5 7 9 8 6 4 2

AUTHOR ACKNOWLEDGMENTS

A tremendous gratitude-filled hug for Antonio Ramos (your advice and support made this possible); El Centro de la Fotografía;
Javier Zapata and everyone in the CARETAS photography department; my family; James Reynolds; the del Barco School for Young Journalists;
the city of Huamanga; my ever-present angels: Pati, Sandra, Susana, Loreto, Carla, Cristy,
my mother, Jenne; and of course my wonderful editor, Cathy Herbert.

DEDICATION: To the little Ayacuchan boys who grew up to be my father and Tío Renan, and to Jesús and Ximena, and all the children of Huamanga.

A CHILD'S DAY
IN A PERUVIAN CITY

Sara Andrea Fajardo

BENCHMARK BOOKS

MARSHALL CAVENDISH
NEW YORK

AUTHOR'S NOTE

Enrique lives in the city of Ayacucho, which is perched on one of the world's tallest mountain ranges, the Andes. If you came to visit Ayacucho, you would notice *caseritas* (street vendors) on every corner: perhaps someone selling homemade yogurt or bread, or a medicine made from snakes and herbs. With all the bustling activity, it is very difficult to sleep late. Most people are up and about before the clock strikes six. Even before this, the city buses and motorcycle taxis are honking their way through the streets.

Enrique's favorite day of the week is Sunday, when most of the shops are closed and Peruvian families spend the day together. Enrique especially looks forward to trips to *el campo*, the countryside, where there are outdoor restaurants that serve delicious food. On days like this Enrique and his family talk about all the things that have happened during the week, and Enrique tells them the latest jokes he has heard at school. On the way back home, he and his little sister, Ximena, do what *Ayacuchanos* (people from Ayacucho) love most—they sing at the top of their voices!

PERU

Ayacucho

SOUTH AMERICA

Jesús Enrique Fernández is seven years old. His family likes to call him "Enriquito," which means "little Enrique."

Enrique lives high up in the Andes Mountains, in the city of Ayacucho, with his parents and his younger sister, Ximena. His father, Jesús, manages the family bakery, and his mother, Maricela, runs the family café.

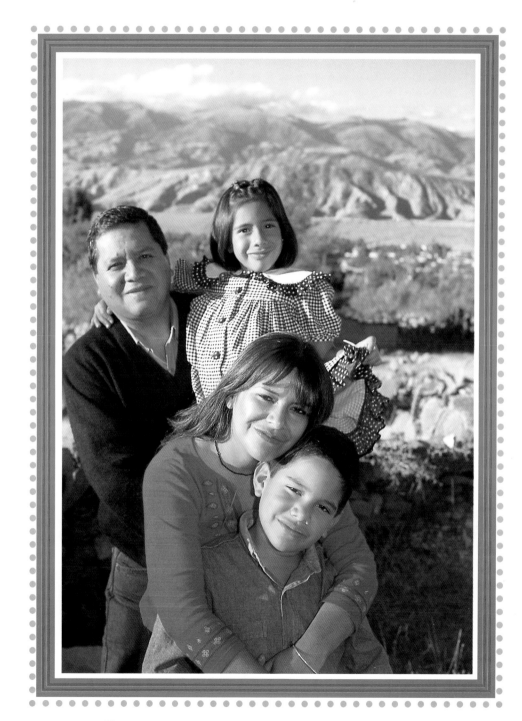

Just before the rooster crows at six-thirty, Enrique is up and ready to start the day. He puts on his school uniform, and his mother helps him comb his hair. Enrique is still yawning as he ties the laces of his shoes, which he polished the night before.

Enrique's first chore of the day is to get the *chaplas* from the corner bakery, where the bakers have been busy working since four o'clock. Nothing goes better with chaplas than *Milo*, a chocolate powder that you stir into hot milk. Enrique loves dipping the crispy chaplas into his milk and making them soggy.

CHAPLAS are a type of flat bread made only in Ayacucho. The ovens used to bake them are usually very old and don't have temperature gauges. The bakers say that they can tell when the oven is hot enough simply by looking at the color of the fire's flames.

By seven-thirty Enrique and his mother are waiting at the street corner to hail one of the hundreds of motorcycle taxis that zip through the streets. Enrique's motorcycle taxi this morning doesn't have a door, so he enjoys feeling the wind on his face as he goes.

No matter what route Enrique takes, he always passes two or three Catholic churches. He can hear the flower and candle sellers calling out to the churchgoers, asking them to buy something for their favorite saint.

Many of the houses and shops that Enrique sees along the way have models of churches, bulls, or musicians on their rooftops. These ceramic sculptures are believed to protect the buildings.

Enrique's *escuela* (school) is a colonial building, like many buildings in the city. He runs through the huge colonial archways in a hurry to greet his friends Quispe, Durand, and Arias.

The colonial buildings of Ayacucho date back to the time when Peru was a colony of Spain. Peru finally broke free from Spain and became independent almost two hundred years ago, in 1824.

The school day always begins with an assembly. All the students sing Peru's national anthem and say a prayer together before going into school.

Enrique attends a Catholic school, so the school prayer is a Catholic one. Most people who live in Ayacucho, and most Peruvians, are Catholic. There are thirty-three Catholic churches in Ayacucho alone!

Señor Livia, Enrique's teacher, starts by taking attendance and checking that the students have remembered their homework. The first lesson is math, Enrique's favorite. Enrique would like to be an astronaut when he grows up, but he knows he needs to pass lots of math tests first.

Enrique and his friends volunteer to go up to the board. Then Señor Livia writes some equations and they have a race to see who can solve the problems the fastest. As usual, Enrique is the first to finish!

It is soon time for *refrigerio* (snack break). Enrique usually eats chaplas for refrigerio, but today his mother gave him money to buy something from the *kiosko* (snack shop). He chooses strawberry-flavored gelatin, which tastes delicious in the late morning sun.

Enrique and his friends are drinking Inca Kola, *Peru's most popular soft drink. Peruvians drink Inca Kola with everything. It tastes especially good with their two favorite foods:* cebiche *(fish cooked with lemon) and* chifa *(Chinese food).*

When refrigerio is over, Enrique has a PE (physical education) lesson. The school is in the middle of a big basketball tournament, and Enrique is learning some new techniques.

At the end of the morning, Enrique's *mami* (mom) picks up Enrique and Ximena and they walk to the market. The buildings that they pass are made out of stone and adobe (bricks molded from mud and straw).

There are so many things to see at *el mercado* (the market) that Enrique doesn't know where to look first.

Many of the market vendors are native *Quechua* people, and wear traditional dress. Quechua women from Ayacucho wear square-shaped white hats and full skirts called *polleras*.

QUECHUA is the name of the South American Indian people who live in this part of Peru. You can tell which town or village a Quechua man comes from by the shape and color of his hat or, if it is a Quechua woman, by the style of her llikllita *(shawl).*

17

The fruit and vegetable section makes Enrique's mouth water. There is a lot to choose from—even black and purple varieties of potato. Today Enrique's mother is looking for an avocado. Enrique picks one that is soft and ready to eat.

El almuerzo (lunch) is the biggest meal of the day in Peru. Ximena orders *chicharrones* (fried pieces of pork), while Enrique and his mother enjoy a typical Andean meal, which includes potatoes, corn, and *cancha* (crunchy, popped corn).

Peru grows more varieties of corn than anywhere else in the world. Researchers have even found corn kernels in Peruvian tombs that are more than a thousand years old. The corn was so well preserved inside the tombs, the researchers said it looked fresh enough to pop.

When they get home, Enrique's mami takes some oranges and glasses of *chicha morada* (a sweet drink made from purple corn) out into the garden. Then they settle down to read some stories together.

Enrique loves playing *futbolín* (table soccer). Every time he scores a goal he shouts "*G-O-O-O-O-L!!!!*" just like they do during matches on television.

Soccer is Peru's national sport. Whenever there is an important match, people paint their faces with the colors of their favorite team and, if their team wins, they celebrate by singing in the streets.

At about five o'clock Enrique's *papi* (dad) takes the children to their favorite place in Ayacucho—Moreno's candy store. Ximena is still little, so she needs her father to lift her up to reach the lollipops. Enrique chooses chocolate-covered cookies.

Every visit to Moreno's candy store is followed by a stroll in the *Plaza de Armas* (town square). Enrique and Ximena run around the statue of *Sucre* and climb the lampposts until their papi says it is time to go home.

SUCRE Antonio José de Sucre was the military general who led the Battle of Ayacucho, the battle that freed Peru from Spanish rule.

Later in the evening there is a procession in honor of the patron saint of Enrique's school, *María Auxiliadora* (Mary, Helper of Christians). Enrique and his school friends have each made a lantern to carry with them as they walk in front of the float.

It takes more than fifty men to carry the float through the streets because it is so heavy. It is made from eucalyptus logs that have been built up into a pyramid, covered with white wax, and then decorated with handmade flowers and candles.

The procession lasts for more than two hours. Afterward Enrique changes out of his school uniform and warms himself with a cup of *café con leche* (milky coffee) at the family's café. Ximena always thinks Enrique's food looks nicer than her own, so Enrique lets her have a bite of his chicken sandwich.

Before bedtime Enrique needs some help with his math homework.
His papi goes through each problem with him, and makes sure that
Enrique understands by asking him lots of questions.

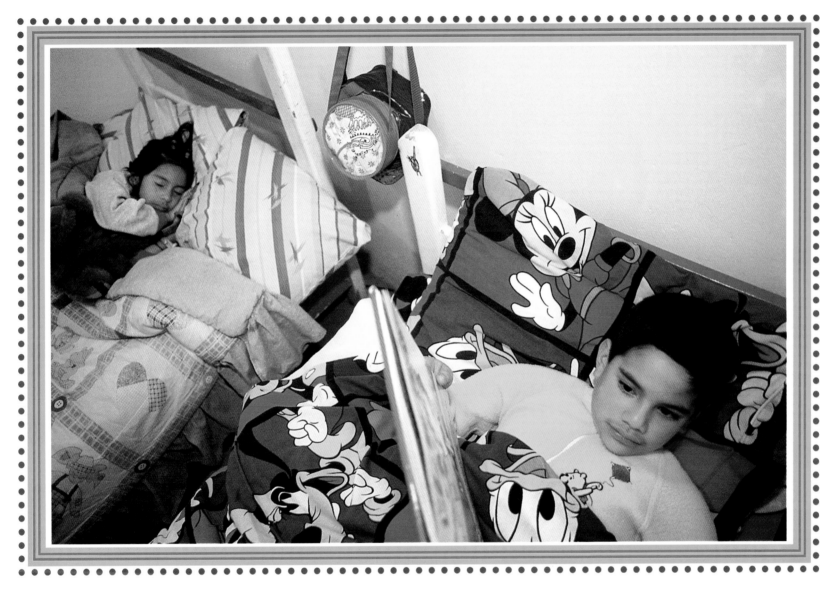

Enrique is very tired after his busy day. He only reads a few lines of his book before whispering good night to his sister and turning off the light. *"Buenas noches, Enrique."* (Good night, Enrique.)

MORE ABOUT PERU

PERU, THE LAND

If you took a bus across Peru you would pass through tropical rainforests, mountains, and deserts. The journey wouldn't be easy. High up in the Andes Mountains, for example, the air is so thin that some visitors have had to wear oxygen masks just to be able to breathe. The Peruvian tropical rainforest offers a very different kind of adventure. Everything that lives there, whether it is an animal, insect, or plant, grows to be enormous. Some species of ant are the size of an adult's thumb!

Peru only has two seasons: wet and dry. People are careful not to get caught in the rain during the wet season because the raindrops are so heavy and fall so quickly that you can be drenched in seconds.

PERU, THE PEOPLE

Every village, town, and city in Peru has one thing in common: a *Plaza de Armas* (town square), where Peruvians go to see and be seen. Each plaza has gardens and walkways for people to enjoy, and usually a fountain or a statue right in the center. Local parades or religious processions always begin and end at the plaza, and the most important buildings in the town are built around this central area.

Peruvians have two passions: family and soccer. Sundays in Peru are set aside especially as a time to spend with the family. Even after people get married, they remain very close to their parents; sometimes people build extensions onto their homes so that they can all continue living together. One of the things Peruvian families enjoy doing together is watching soccer. The whole country seems to come to a standstill when the Peruvian national team plays because everyone stops what he or she is doing to watch the match!

Despite all the things Peruvians have in common, every town in the country is unique, with its own food, traditions, music, and clothing. Communities that are only separated by a few miles will each offer something different, whether this is a special cheese, candy, or the little wooden boxes filled with carvings of famous Andeans, that are made in Ayacucho.

PERU, THE PAST

Ancient Peru was the birthplace of a series of advanced and brilliant cultures that eventually came together in the glorious Inca Empire. The people of the Inca Empire worshiped the sun god, Inti. They built large stone temples in his honor, which they decorated with gold. The Inca himself (the emperor) was believed to be a descendant of Inti, and wore splendid robes encrusted with gold jewelry and precious stones.

So when the Spanish conquistador (conqueror) Francisco Pizarro and his men arrived in Peru in 1531, they must have felt that they had discovered a golden land. The Inca Empire fell under Spanish rule, and Peru became known as the Pearl of the Spanish Empire. It wasn't until 1824 that Peru broke free from Spain and became independent. Peru is now a modern democratic nation, but the ancient ruins you can see wherever you go are a constant reminder of the country's rich and interesting past.

RELIGION IN PERU

Most Peruvians are Roman Catholic—the religion that was brought to Peru by the Spanish. However, Peruvians are still heavily influenced by the beliefs of their ancient ancestors. They often talk about the earth goddess *Pacha Mama*, and it is a custom in the Andes to pour a bit of your drink on the ground as an offering to the earth.

LANGUAGE IN PERU

Most Peruvians speak Spanish, the language of Peruvian television, newspapers, books, and politics; but many other languages are spoken around the country. Of these Quechua is the most widespread. The people of Ayacucho are nearly all bilingual—they speak both Spanish and Quechua.

All Peruvian children learn and study in Spanish at school. In some towns where Spanish is not the main language, the townspeople want their children to be taught in the local language as well. There have been cases where teachers sent by the government have been asked to leave because they were not able to teach in the local language.

Peruvians can tell which region people come from by the way they speak Spanish. People from Ayacucho have a soft, almost whispery way of speaking, while people from the tropical rainforest speak in a singsong fashion.

Even though Spanish has the same alphabet as English, many letters are pronounced differently. Spanish writing uses accents and a letter that looks like an English "n," only with a mustache on top: "ñ" (pronounced like the "ny" in "canyon").

SOME SPANISH WORDS AND PHRASES:
hola (oh-la)—hello
adios (a-dee-ohs)—goodbye
gracias (grah-see-ahs)—thank you
¿Cómo te llamas? (*coh*-moh tay ya-mas)—
    What is your name?

SOME QUECHUA WORDS AND PHRASES:
allinllachu (ah-yeen-*ya*-chue)—hello
qayakama (ha-ya-*kah*-mah)—good-bye
pakrasunki (pock-rah-*soon*-key)—thank you
Imataq sutiki? (ee-*mah*-tock sue-*tee*-key)—
    What is your name?

THE SPANISH AND QUECHUA WORDS IN THE BOOK

el almuerzo–lunch

Ayacuchanos–the people who live in Ayacucho

Buenas noches–Good night

café con leche–milky coffee

el campo–the countryside

cancha–crunchy, popped corn

caseritas–street vendors

cebiche–fish cooked with lemon

chaplas–flat bread made from flour, water,
   and yeast

chicha morada–a sweet drink made from
   purple corn

chicharrones–fried pieces of pork

chifa–Chinese food

escuela–school

futbolín–table soccer

gol–goal

Inca Kola–Peru's national soft drink

kiosko–snack shop

llikllita–shawl

mami–mom

María Auxiliadora–Mary, Helper of Christians,
   the patron saint of Enrique's school

el mercado–the market

Milo–a chocolate powder that you can stir into
   hot milk to make a delicious drink

Pacha Mama–Mother Earth

papi–dad

Plaza de Armas–town square

polleras–the skirts worn by the Quechua women
   of Ayacucho

Quechua–the South American Indian people
   who live in the Andes Mountains.
   Quechua is also the name of the language
   they speak.

refrigerio–snack break

Sucre–the military general who led the Battle
   of Ayacucho in 1824. Sucre's victory meant that
   Peru and South America were freed from
   Spanish rule.

FIND OUT MORE

Allard, Denise. *Peru*. Austin, Texas: Raintree Steck-Vaughn, 1997.

Kalman, Bobbie. *Peru: The People and Culture*. Madison, Wisconsin: Turtleback Books, 1994.

Thoennes, Kristin. *Peru*. Mankato, Minnesota: Capstone Press, 1999.

INDEX